STUDY GUIDE

THE INVISIBLE WAR

WHAT EVERY BELIEVER NEEDS TO KNOW ABOUT SATAN, DEMONS & SPIRITUAL WARFARE

CHIP INGRAM

Printed in the U.S.A. For more information go to livingontheedge.org or email info@lote.org.

CONTENTS

BEFORE YOU BEGIN

Way to go! The fact that you have this Bible study in your hands proves that you care about your spiritual life, especially in light of the invisible war we face as Christians.

Many believers have no idea how much of their daily life is influenced by the subtle deception and lies of our adversary. This study will help you prepare yourself for spiritual battle, cultivate invincible faith, and find freedom from demonic influence.

Here are some helpful tips for your journey:

- Set a time and place for your study and guard it.
- Pray! Ask God to protect you and give you insight, persistence, and courage.
- Ask reliable and spiritually mature friends to pray for you and to hold you accountable.
- Seek out your pastor or a spiritual mentor if you encounter anything you don't understand.

I'm confident that the Invisible War Bible study will help you understand your power and position in Christ and how to practically put on the full armor of God and stand firm against the enemy!

Praying for your spiritual growth,

CHIP INGRAM
CEO and Teaching Pastor, Living on the Edge

HOW TO GET THE MOST OUT OF THIS STUDY

Each of the eight sessions in this video-based Bible study is designed with three sections to help you on your journey.

1. TAKE IT IN

Watch Chip Ingram's video teaching and follow along with the outline provided. Jot down an exclamation point next to something that really stands out to you. Add details from the video, and underline thoughts and topics you want to learn more about. Reading from your own Bible will allow you to make notes in it and find other passages that might be relevant to the study.

2. THINK IT OVER

After you watch the video teaching, take some time to dig deeper and process your response. Work through the four to six questions in each session to unpack some of the key principles and passages that Chip taught. Write your responses in the lines provided, so that you can revisit, remember, and reflect on what God has taught you through this study.

3. LIVE IT OUT

The point of your study is not just to gain knowledge. It's to grow in your knowledge of who God is and how He wants you to live so that you can serve Him better. That's why each session ends with suggested action steps to help you apply what you've learned. These include prompts for prayer, reflection, journaling, Scripture meditation, and memorization.

THE INVISIBLE WAR

SESSION 1

What Is the Invisible War?

EPHESIANS 6:10-12

TAKE IT IN

Finally, ***be strong in the Lord*** *and in the strength of His might.* ***Put on the full armor of God****, so that you will be able to stand firm against the schemes of the devil. For our struggle is not against flesh and blood, but against the rulers, against the powers, against the world forces of this darkness, against the spiritual forces of wickedness in the heavenly places.*

EPHESIANS 6:10-12 NASB

Be Strong   Put on Full Armor ______ **command**

Allow yourself to be continually strengthened by the power already made available to you. (Ephesians 6:10)

Allow yourself to be continually strengthened by the power already made available to you in your new position in Christ and your relationship with him. The power that raised Christ from the dead now also dwells in you.

Put on full armor ______ **command**

Finally, be strong in the Lord and in the strength of His might. Put on the full armor of God, so that you will be able to stand firm against the ***schemes*** *of the devil. For our* ***struggle*** *is not against flesh and blood, but against the rulers, against the powers, against the world forces of this darkness, against the spiritual forces of wickedness in the heavenly places.*

EPHESIANS 6:10-12 NASB

By continually and repeatedly putting on, at specific points in time, the spiritual protection God has provided for you, for the express purpose of holding on to your position in Christ as you are bombarded by satanic strategies designed to destroy you and/or render you ineffective in kingdom pursuits. (Ephesians 6:11)

The ____________________ for the commands

It's because our real **struggle** (battle, wrestling match to the death) is not against physical/material adversaries (people, circumstances, organizations) but against a hierarchy of demonic forces doing battle in the spiritual realm. (Ephesians 6:12)

Five Basic Truths About Spiritual Warfare

1. **There is an ____________________________ world that is just as real as the visible world.** (Ephesians 6:12)
   - Old Testament – 2 Kings 6:15-19
   - New Testament – 2 Corinthians 10:3-5

2. **We are involved in an invisible _____________, a cosmic conflict that has eternal implications.** (Ephesians 6:12)

For though we walk in the flesh, we do not war according to the flesh, for the weapons of our warfare are not of the flesh, but divinely powerful for the destruction of fortresses. We are destroying speculations and every lofty thing raised up against the knowledge of God, and we are taking every thought captive to the obedience of Christ.

2 CORINTHIANS 10:3-5 NASB

90% of the battles we face in spiritual warfare are in our hearts and our minds.

> *. . . in whose case the god of this world has blinded the minds of the unbelieving so that they might not see the light of the gospel of the glory of Christ, who is the image of God.*
>
> 2 CORINTHIANS 4:4 NASB

People not believing in Christ is not primarily an intellectual issue. It's a moral issue. It's not that people don't understand, but there is an enemy blinding people from understanding and making the connection

There is a correlation between praying and beseeching God, asking the Father to cause His Spirit to work in the heart of someone to open their eyes and open their mind where they could lay down their pride, or feeling unworthy in order to believe and to trust in what Christ has provided.

THINK IT OVER

1. What is the first thought that comes to mind when you hear the phrase "spiritual warfare"? After watching today's teaching, has your perspective of spiritual warfare changed? If yes, how did it change?

____

____

____

____

____

____

2. C. S. Lewis said that the greatest error when it comes to spiritual warfare is to think far too much about Satan or to think far too little about him. What do you think "far too much" and "far too little" look like? Where do you fall on this spectrum?

3. When was the last time you honestly considered that a struggle or relational conflict was rooted in satanic opposition?

4. Chip says, "It's not that people don't understand, but there is an enemy blinding people from understanding and making the connection." Do you agree? Why or why not?

5. The Apostle Paul tells us in 2 Corinthians 10:5 to take "every thought captive to the obedience of Christ." What do you think the he means by that?

LIVE IT OUT

1. Pray and ask God for His help in identifying and overcoming struggles or relational conflicts that could be rooted in satanic opposition.

"Lord Jesus, thank You that I fight from victory because You have already won. You are the almighty, all-powerful, all-knowing and all-loving God! Help me find my strength in You and in Your might. Help me put on the full armor of God so that I may be able to stand firm against the schemes of the devil. I need Your wisdom to understand Satan and his schemes. Remind me that my struggle is not against flesh and blood but against the rulers, against the powers, against the world forces of this darkness, against the spiritual forces of wickedness in the heavenly places. Protect me and give me courage to follow You and what You would have me do. Thank You for loving me. I love You. In Jesus' name, amen."

---

2. Chip shares that although spiritual warfare can be overt, 90% of the battle is in our hearts and minds.

   - Take time to reflect on your thought life. What influences your thought life?

   - Do you believe that some of your thoughts are coming from the work of spiritual forces of wickedness? (This could take the form of twisted truths, straight-out lies, or heavyheartedness about your identity, worth, purpose, work, relationships, etc.)

- What thoughts do you need to take "captive to the obedience of Christ"? List those thoughts here.

- Chip talks about how writing truths on cards helps him renew his mind and take every thought captive. Replace the thoughts you listed above with the truth of Scripture. Write out the verses on 3x5 cards and place them where you can read them when the lies attack you.

EXAMPLE

Lie:

You are a nobody. How could anyone love you?

Truth:

John 3:16: For God so loved the world that he gave his one and only Son, that whoever believes in him shall not perish but have eternal life. (NIV)

Ephesians 3:17b-19a: ...and that you, being rooted and grounded in love, may be able to comprehend with all the saints what is the breadth and length and height and depth, and to know the love of Christ which surpasses knowledge. (NASB)

3. Pray and ask God to help you identify the lies that are aimed at you, remember the truth, and move closer to Him.

THE INVISIBLE WAR

SESSION 2

Who Are We Fighting?

EPHESIANS 6:10-12

TAKE IT IN

Five Basic Truths About Spiritual Warfare

(continued)

3. Our foe is ______________________________ and his goal is to destroy us and discredit the cause of Christ. (Ephesians 6:12)

Be of sober spirit, be on the alert. Your adversary, the devil, prowls around like a roaring lion, seeking someone to devour.

1 PETER 5:8 NASB

But Michael the archangel, when he disputed with the devil and argued about the body of Moses, did not dare pronounce against him a railing judgment, but said, "The Lord rebuke you!"

JUDE 1:9 NASB

The enemy will do things in your life to give fear at the depth of your soul that will paralyze you and keep you from trusting God and doing His will.

Is Satan for real?

- Authority of the Bible *Genesis 3:1; 1 Chronicles 21:1; Revelation 12:9*
- Testimony of Christ *Matthew 4*

Who is Satan?

- A created spirit *Colossians 1:16*
- An angel *Matthew 25:41; Revelation 12:7*
- A cherub *Ezekiel 28:14*
- Highest of all created beings *Ezekiel 28:14; Jude 1:6*

Where did Satan come from?

- Created perfect *Ezekiel 28:12-13*
- Had heavenly estate *Jude 1:6*
- Guardian of God's glory *Ezekiel 28:14*
- Occasion of his sin = power and beauty *Ezekiel 28*
- Nature of his sin = pride *1 Timothy 3:6; Isaiah 14:13*
- Cause of his sin = personal free choice *James 1:13-14*

Satan's Five "I Will" Statements (Isaiah 14:13-14)

1. I will ascend to heaven.
2. I will raise my throne above the stars of God.
3. I will sit on the mount of the assembly.
4. I will ascend above the heights of the clouds.
5. I will make myself like the Most High.

"Part of the problem with our faith today is that we do not truly believe in the reality of the spiritual, either the good side or the evil side. In our world people maintain their sense of respectability by rejecting everything except what they can see in the natural world. To accept that there is more than that threatens their self-identity as proper, intelligent citizens of the modern world."

Dallas Willard, *Life Without Lack*, page 68

4. We must ____________________ our foe, but not fear him—become acutely aware of his "methods," but not be preoccupied by them. (Ephesians 6:11)

...so that no advantage would be taken of us by Satan, for we are not ignorant of his ***schemes****.*

2 CORINTHIANS 2:11 NASB

Satan's names reveal his ___________________________.

- Prince of the World *John 12:31*
- Satan (adversary) *Job 1:6-7; 1 Thessalonians 2:18*
- Lucifer (son of the morning)

- Evil One *1 John 5:19*
- Tempter *1 Thessalonians 3:5*
- Deceiver
- Accuser of the brethren
- Devil (slanderer) *1 Peter 5:8*
- Beelzebub, Ruler of the Demons *Matthew 12:24*
- Belial *2 Corinthians 6:15*
- Representations include:
    - Serpent *Genesis 3*
    - Dragon *Revelation 12:3*
    - Angel of Light *2 Corinthians 11:14*

Satan attacks God's people, the Church, by . . .

- False philosophies *Colossians 2:8*
- False religions *1 Corinthians 10:19*
- False ministers *2 Corinthians 11:14-15*
- False doctrine *1 John 2:18*
- False disciples *Matthew 13:24-30*
- False morals *2 Thessalonians 2:7-8*

Satan attacks God's program by . . .

- Directing governments *Daniel 10:13*
- Deceiving man *2 Corinthians 4:4*
- Destroying life *Hebrews 2:14-15*
- Persecuting the saints *Revelation 2:10*
- Preventing service *1 Thessalonians 2:18*
- Promoting schisms *2 Corinthians 2:10-11*
- Planting doubt *Genesis 3:1-5*
- Provoking sin:
    - Anger *Ephesians 4:26-27*
    - Pride *1 Timothy 3:6*
    - Worry *Matthew 13:22*
    - Self-reliance *1 Chronicles 21:1*
    - Discouragement *1 Peter 5:6-8*
    - Worldliness *1 John 2:16*
    - Lying *Acts 5:3*
    - Immorality *1 Corinthians 5:1-2*
- Producing sects/cults *1 Timothy 4:1*

Satan's power is ________________________.

- He is created, therefore not omniscient or infinite.
- He can be resisted by the Christian. *James 4:7*
- God places limitation on him. *Job 1:12*

Balance and wisdom are crucial in our assessment of spiritual opposition. To assign too much or too little credit to the reality of demonic activity is to err greatly.

As believers in Christ, we do not fight for victory; we fight ________________ victory. In Christ's power, we are invincible. (Ephesians 6:10)

Promises from God Concerning Victory over Satan

You are from God, little children, and have overcome them; because greater is He who is in you than he who is in the world.

1 JOHN 4:4 NASB

For whatever is born of God overcomes the world; and this is the victory that has overcome the world—our faith. Who is the one who overcomes the world, but he who believes that Jesus is the Son of God?

1 JOHN 5:4-5 NASB

They triumphed over him by the blood of the Lamb and by the word of their testimony; they did not love their lives so much as to shrink from death.

REVELATION 12:11 NIV

Submit therefore to God. Resist the devil and he will flee from you.

JAMES 4:7 NASB

SUMMARY

1. **Satan is a ______________________________ foe.** *John 12:31*

2. **Jesus ______________________________ the works of the devil.** *Colossians 2:14*

3. **We are ______________________________ in Christ.** *1 Corinthians 15:55-58*

4. **We have the ____________________ and resources to resist Satan and demonic attacks.** *1 John 4:4*

5. **We must ________________ how to put on the full armor of God to experience the victory that we already possess.**

THINK IT OVER

1. Someone once said, "The best crime Satan ever perpetrated was to convince the world he does not exist." Do you agree? Why or why not?

____

____

____

____

____

____

____

____

____

2. Peter tells us in 1 Peter 5:8, "Be alert and of sober mind. Your enemy the devil prowls around like a roaring lion looking for someone to devour." What does Peter describe Satan as? How does his strong warning change how you view Satan?

3. We learned in today's teaching that Satan's names reveal his strategies. Which of Satan's names and strategies stand out to you? Why?

4. Satan strategically attacks God's people and God's program. Quickly review the ways Satan attacks God's people. Which areas do you think the church is most prone to attack? Why?

5. Which of the four victory promises from God gives you the most hope? Why?

____

____

____

____

____

____

LIVE IT OUT

MEMORIZE THESE VERSES:

Submit therefore to God. Resist the devil and he will flee from you.

JAMES 4:7 NASB

You are from God, little children, and have overcome them; because greater is He who is in you than he who is in the world.

1 JOHN 4:4 NASB

Chip tells us, "You're in a battle, and the battle is for your soul. God wants to use you like no one else in the world. He's uniquely put you in a place and given you gifts. The enemy wants to distract you and get you thinking about everything or anything that keeps you from being a daughter or a son who's becoming more and more like Christ."

What is Satan's game plan to distract and defeat you? How are you going to fight back in victory? Share with a trusted friend what you are learning, and ask for their help in keeping you alert, sober minded, and accountable.

THE INVISIBLE WAR

SESSION 3

Four Keys to Spiritual Victory

EPHESIANS 6:13-15

TAKE IT IN

The South Pacific After World War II Was Won

- Pockets of guerrilla warfare continued on hundreds of islands.
- The victory had been won, but battles continued and lives were lost; the bullets were real.
- The same is true spiritually:

  1. Satan was defeated at the cross.
  2. Sin's penalty was paid for all time for all people.
  3. Sin's power was broken.
  4. Yet Satan and his host of fallen angels engage in guerrilla warfare to discourage, deceive, divide, and destroy God's people and God's program.
  5. Believers are commanded to equip and prepare themselves in the strength of the Lord and in His mighty power to stand firm against the enemy's schemes, repel his multifaceted attacks, and engage and defeat him in specific battles. *Ephesians 6:10-12*

The Question: How does this work?

The Answer: Four Keys to Spiritual Victory

1. We must become ______________ of the battle.
2. We must learn to ___________________________ God's protection for daily living.

3. We must learn to ______________________ the enemy with supernatural weapons.

4. We must ______________________ God's means of deliverance when spiritual attack occurs.

How Can You Prepare Yourself for Satanic Attack?

Therefore, take up the full armor of God, so that you will be able to resist in the evil day, and having done everything, to stand firm. Stand firm therefore, having girded your loins with truth, and having put on the breastplate of righteousness, and having shod your feet with the preparation of the gospel of peace.

EPHESIANS 6:13-15 NASB

Ephesians 6:13

- Our commander (Jesus Christ) urgently commands us to pick up our spiritual armor and put it on.
  Why? - For the purpose of being fully prepared and enabled to withstand the grave and difficult dark times when the enemy attacks.

H- ______________________

A- ______________________

L- ______________________

T- ______________________

We're commanded to consciously and vigorously make a decisive act to stand our ground firmly and fearlessly against the enemy's assaults as he seeks to deceive, accuse, and discourage us.

Ephesians 6:14a

- After picking up our armor in preparation for battle, we are then commanded to consciously and vigorously make a decisive act (or succession of acts) to stand our ground firmly and fearlessly against the enemy's assaults as he seeks to deceive, accuse, and discourage us.

Ephesians 6:14b-15

- Using the metaphor of a Roman soldier's armor (which protected him in battle), we are given three specific pieces of spiritual armor that must be "put on" by us as believers as a prerequisite to standing firmly and fearlessly against demonic attack.

"**Having girded your loins with ____________________**"

- Truth: Candor, sincerity, truthfulness rooted in the objective reality of the truth of God's Word, but here refers to the subjective practical application of openness and honesty in all things with God and men.

- Satan's first attack on mankind was deception, which was followed by man's hiding, denial, and blame-shifting.

- The belt of truth is the man or woman whose mind will practice no deceit and attempt no disguises in their walk with God. – Kenneth S. Wuest

The prerequisite is that we are ______________________.

Search me, O God, and know my heart; try me and know my anxious thoughts; and see if there be any hurtful way in me, and lead me in the everlasting way.

PSALM 139:23-24 NASB

The Lord is near to the brokenhearted
And saves those who are crushed in spirit.

PSALM 34:18 NASB

The Lord is near to all who call upon Him,
To all who call upon Him in truth.

PSALM 145:18 NASB

THINK IT OVER

1. In today's teaching, Chip shares the acronym HALT, the four predictable times in every human being's life when temptation will feel more powerful. Have you found this to be true as well? In which of the four predictable times are you most vulnerable? How will being more aware help you be less vulnerable?

2. What new insight did you gain about the belt of truth?

3. Chip's definition of the belt of truth is being honest with God, being honest with yourself, and being honest with others. Why is it so important to be honest, especially in light of Satan's primary tactic of deception?

4. In what ways have you been less than honest with yourself? Can you think of one specific instance in which you were less than honest and justified your choice? What was the result?

5. Chip says, "We tend to think that God always looks at our history, and I think God looks at the intent of our hearts. We mess up, but when we're humble, genuine, and vulnerable and ask for forgiveness, He is a God who lovingly forgives. We don't have to twist His arm for Him to be merciful. He longs to not give you what you deserve. He longs to give you grace. He longs to do whatever is necessary to forgive and to restore and to pull His children back close to Him." Does this view of God and His loving grace change the way you seek Him in your failures? How?

____

____

____

____

____

____

LIVE IT OUT

God always looks at the heart for two reasons. First, our heart is the source of our actions and life. But second—and more important—our thoughts are where Satan implies his trade. He governs through images, through ideas, through feelings and fears. From this complex arena of our minds and our hearts comes most of our actions, and this is where Satan focuses his tasks.

Above all else, guard your heart, for everything you do flows from it.

PROVERBS 4:23 NIV

David knew he needed God's help to be honest with himself, God, and others. He asked God to search and know his heart. Follow David's example by asking God to search your heart, test it, and reveal to you what He finds.

PRAY

Search me, O God, and know my heart;
Try me and know my anxious thoughts;
And see if there be any hurtful way in me,
And lead me in the everlasting way.

PSALM 139:23-24 NASB

- How is my thought life?
- What lies am I buying into?
- How are the lies I believe affecting my life and others?
- Have I hurt anyone?

As God shows you sin, confess it and ask for His forgiveness. Seek His help in leading you into the way everlasting. Once you have made peace with God, if there is someone you have hurt, go and make peace with them.

THE INVISIBLE WAR

SESSION 4

How to Prepare Yourself for Spiritual Battle

EPHESIANS 6:13-15

TAKE IT IN

How Can You Prepare Yourself for Satanic Attack?

(continued)

2. "Having put on the breastplate of ________________________."

- Righteousness: Uprightness, right living, integrity in one's lifestyle and character—conforming of our will with God's will. Although rooted in the object righteousness that we already possess in our standing before God through the work of Christ, this breastplate of righteousness is the practical application of the truth to our lives.

- Satan's attacks are not merely deception but also accusation (resulting in guilt and condemnation) of the believer. When we willfully turn away from what we know is God's will, we open ourselves to satanic attack.

The breastplate of righteousness is the ________________________ of the truth for your life.

- Old Testament: Saul

- New Testament: Peter

APPLICATION

Therefore, to one who knows the right thing to do and does not do it, to him it is sin.

JAMES 4:17 NASB

Conviction is very ____________________, and the goal is to ____________________ you to your heavenly Father.

Condemnation is ____________________ and makes you feel ____________________ and makes you want to go away from your heavenly Father.

- Anyone you need to forgive?
- Any unresolved relationships?
- Any issues with purity in your thoughts? In your speech?
- Any issues in your finances?
- Are your priorities where you think they need to be?
- Are there any habits you need to change?

3. "Having shod your feet with the preparation of the gospel of ____________________"

- Preparation: Establishment, the means of a firm foundation, and also conveys the idea of readiness to share the gospel, which brings peace between man and God.

- Satan not only uses deception and condemnation to neutralize believers but also specializes in casting doubt on the very basis of God's goodness and the means by which we have received it: the Gospel.

Now I make known to you, brethren, the gospel which I preached to you, which also you received, in which also you stand, by which also you are saved, if you hold fast the word which I preached to you, unless you believed in vain.

For I delivered to you as of first importance what I also received, that Christ died for our sins according to the Scriptures, and that He was buried, and that He was raised on the third day according to the Scriptures, and that He appeared to Cephas, then to the twelve. After that He appeared to more than five hundred brethren at one time, most of whom remain until now, but some have fallen asleep; then He appeared to James, then to all the apostles; and last of all, as to one untimely born, He appeared to me also.

1 CORINTHIANS 15:1-8 NASB

APPLICATION

1. Know and understand the content of the gospel.
   1 Corinthians 15:1-5; Ephesians 2:1-9

2. Know the basis for your eternal security and the assurance of your salvation.
   Security *Romans 8:38; Ephesians 1:13-14*
   Assurance *1 John 5:13*

3. Faith is based on facts, not feelings.

4. Sharing your faith is one of the most powerful faith builders available. Often the best defense is a good offense.

THINK IT OVER

1. Chip describes the breastplate of righteousness as conforming our will to God's will. It is integrity and character in one's lifestyle. How does conforming your will to God's will protect your heart? Can you think of an example of this in your life?

2. Although conforming to God's will protects our hearts, we still may choose to turn away, which opens us up to attack. Why do you think it is hard for us to choose God's will? Why is it personally challenging for you to choose God's will?

3. Christians often get condemnation and conviction confused. What is the difference between the two? How does the enemy use condemnation to attack you? How does the Holy Spirit use conviction in your life?

4. Are you knowingly or unknowingly living with low-grade guilt and low-grade condemnation? If so, how is it impacting your life?

5. Read Romans 8:1: "Therefore there is now no condemnation for those who are in Christ Jesus." As one who belongs to Christ, are you condemned?

6. Think of a time in the last two weeks that the Holy Spirit living in you convicted you of sin. How did you respond? What truth does John share with us about God's forgiveness in 1 John 1:9? Do you genuinely believe you are forgiven by God?

If we confess our sins, He is faithful and righteous to forgive us our sins and to cleanse us from all unrighteousness.

1 JOHN 1:9 NASB

LIVE IT OUT

Faith is rooted in facts, not feelings. There will be days you don't feel so good about God, and there will be days you don't feel close to Him. Those feelings do not change the facts about your eternal security in Jesus.

Meditate on John 3:16, Romans 6:23, John 10:28-29, Romans 8:38-39, Ephesians 1:13-14, and 1 John 5:11-13. Write out the facts of your eternal security in Jesus Christ and place them in a spot where you will see them regularly. When your feelings dip and doubts arise, read through these verses.

PRAY

"Lord, thank You for being kind, compassionate, slow to anger, abounding in love, and a Father who longs to forgive and restore. I ask that You grant me Your grace to be open and honest with You. Help me to understand the absolute stability and firmness of my eternal security in Jesus because doubts are bombarding my mind. Give me a fresh mindfulness to respond to Your conviction when You point out something in my life. Pull me close to You and restore me. In Christ's name, amen."

Chip believes that sharing your faith is one of the most powerful faith builders available. Take some time to write down your faith story (your life before Jesus, when you accepted Him as your personal Savior, and your life as you walk with Him as His child). Share your faith story with someone this week.

THE INVISIBLE WAR

SESSION 5

Engaging the Enemy

EPHESIANS 6:16-17

TAKE IT IN

Four Facts You Need to Know

FACT #1
God has objectively defeated Satan and his agenda. He has delivered us from sin's penalty and power and ultimately will deliver us from sin's very presence. In the interim, we are involved in guerrilla warfare with demonic forces.

FACT #2
As believers, we have been transferred from the kingdom of darkness to the kingdom of light with all the rights, privileges, and position that being a child of God entails.

FACT #3
The spiritual battle we fight involves a responsibility on our part to "put on" the spiritual protection that God has provided for us. We can and will resist the enemy's attempts to deceive, accuse, and cast doubt when we stand firm against him by:

1. Being honest with God, ourselves, and others as a prerequisite to all spiritual battle.

2. Responding to the truth that God shows us about His will for our lives: righteous living.

3. Having a clear understanding of the gospel and sharing it.

FACT #4
The great majority of spiritual warfare never need go beyond the regular practice of living out our position in Christ by faith. Our practice of Paul's metaphor of the spiritual armor protects us from Satan's ongoing attempts to break our fellowship with Jesus and, as a result, greatly minimizes any impact by the enemy.

There are times when we must move beyond "standing firm" and ____________________ the enemy in actual combat:

- When you're taking significant steps of faith for spiritual growth
- When you've invading enemy territory
- When you're exposing the enemy for who he really is
- When you repent and make a clean break with the world, long-held sin patterns, or unholy relationships
- When God is preparing us (individually or corporately) for great works for His glory

THE QUESTION

When you're wearing your spiritual armor and yet feel yourself bombarded by spiritual opposition, *how do you engage the enemy and win the battle?*

THE ANSWER

. . . in addition to all, taking up the shield of faith with which you will be able to extinguish all the flaming arrows of the evil one. And take the helmet of salvation, and the sword of the Spirit, which is the word of God.

EPHESIANS 6:16-17 NASB

HOW TO ENGAGE THE ENEMY AND WIN

1. "Taking up the shield of____________________"

Faith in this context is our absolute confidence in God, His promises, His power, and His program for our lives.

Although rooted in the objective reality of the gospel and our new standing with God (justification) through Christ (saving faith), this faith refers to our *"present faith in the Lord Jesus for victory over sin and the host of demonic forces" (Kenneth Weust).*

Its purpose: to quench all the fiery missiles of the evil one.

Fiery darts/missiles: The schemes, temptations, lies, deceptions, and attacks aimed at us, God's people, to get us to shift our trust to something or someone other than God (i.e., blasphemous thoughts, hateful thoughts, doubts, burning desire to sin, questioning others' motives, waves of discouragement or depression); often rooted in lies about God's identity or our new identity in Christ.

- Classic Examples *Genesis 3; Matthew 4*

Do not love the world nor the things in the world. If anyone loves the world, the love of the Father is not in him. For all that is in the world, the lust of the flesh and the lust of the eyes and the boastful pride of life, is not from the Father, but is from the world. The world is passing away, and also its lusts; but the one who does the will of God lives forever.

1 JOHN 2:15-17 NASB

THINK IT OVER

1. We began our study today by looking at four facts regarding spiritual warfare. Which fact did you find the most helpful? Why?

2. Standing firm against the enemy's fiery darts is vital, but there are times when we must move beyond standing firm and engage the enemy. Chip gives us five examples of when he believes we must engage. Have you seen this to be true in your own life? If so, which times do you find yourself the most engaged in actual combat?

3. After listening to the teaching today, can you look back and see the enemy's "classic methodology" played out on you? How? What was the result?

4. How can understanding the enemy's methods to shift your trust away from God help you engage the enemy and win? Can you think of a specific example from your life?

5. There are three areas of temptation that we ALL face listed in 1 John 2:16. What are they? How would you describe them in your own words? Is there one that you are more susceptible to believing that it will satisfy you? What would it look like to trust God with it instead of trying to manage it yourself?

LIVE IT OUT

Study the enemy's tactics in the two Scripture passages below. Observe when, where, and how each person was tempted by the enemy.

- Genesis 3
- Matthew 4:1-11

What consistencies do you see in these passages?

How did Jesus respond differently than Adam and Eve?

How can you respond the next time one of these methods is used on you?

MEMORIZE 1 JOHN 2:15-17

Do not love the world nor the things in the world. If anyone loves the world, the love of the Father is not in him. For all that is in the world, the lust of the flesh and the lust of the eyes and the boastful pride of life, is not from the Father, but is from the world. The world is passing away, and also its lusts; but the one who does the will of God lives forever.

THE INVISIBLE WAR

SESSION 6

Winning the War

EPHESIANS 6:16-17

TAKE IT IN

How to Engage the Enemy and Win

(continued)

1. "Taking up the shield of faith."

- **Trusting in God's** ______________________. God has my best in mind.

For the Lord God is a sun and shield;
The Lord gives grace and glory; no good thing
does He withhold from those who walk uprightly.

PSALM 84:11 NASB

- **Trusting in God's** ______________________ **and His Word**. He will accomplish what concerns me.

God is not a man, that He should lie,
Nor a son of man, that He should repent;
Has He said, and will He not do it? Or has
He spoken, and will He not make it good?

NUMBERS 23:19 NASB

- **Trusting in God's** ______________________ **and timing**. His ways are not always easiest, but they're always best.

"For I know the plans that I have for you," declares the
Lord, "plans for welfare and not for calamity to give
you a future and a hope."

JEREMIAH 29:11 NASB

No temptation has overtaken you but such as is common to man; and God is faithful, who will not allow you to be tempted beyond what you are able, but with the temptation will provide the way of escape also, so that you will be able to endure it.

1 CORINTHIANS 10:13 NASB

2. "And take the helmet of ______________________"

- Definition:
    1. Obvious allusion to the security we have as saved, justified believers, safe from Satan's attacks. Focus on present deliverance from sin!

    2. The helmet of salvation is the certainty of deliverance from sin and the protection of our minds in the battle.

- It's not something you can do or receive; it's something you must allow God to do in your mind.

- How? By renewing your mind. *John 17:17; Colossians 3:2; Romans 8:5-8; 12:2*

- Practically: prayer, worship, music, Scripture teaching, Scripture memory, and fellowship.

- Paul calls the helmet our hope (certainty) of God's deliverance. *1 Thessalonians 5:8*

APPLICATION

Christians who are not filling their minds with Scripture are like warriors going out to battle without a helmet.

3. "And take the sword of the ________________________"
Ephesians 6:17

- Definition: The sword of the Spirit is the Word (*rhema*—spoken word, or words given to us by the Spirit of God), to do close, hand-to-hand combat with the lies and deceptions of the enemy. The truth of God's Word quoted and applied to the specific lie or deception of the enemy will allow you to take "every thought captive to the obedience of Christ" (2 Corinthians 10:5).

APPLICATION

Jesus models for us the use of the sword of the Spirit.
Matthew 4:1-11

- Implications for us. *Psalm 119:105; 19:9-11*

- Practical considerations—note that the sword is both a defensive and an offensive weapon.

For the word of God is living and active and sharper than any two-edged sword, and piercing as far as the division of soul and spirit, of both joints and marrow, and able to judge the thoughts and intentions of the heart.

HEBREWS 4:12 NASB

SUMMARY: How to Engage the Enemy in Spiritual Warfare

1. Prerequisite is a ____________________ spiritual life.

2. Understand your ____________________ in Christ.

3. ____________________ when demonic influence may be the cause.

4. Claim God's promises ____________________.

5. Take our authority and position in Christ and ____________________ demonic forces to cease their activity and depart.

THINK IT OVER

1. When the fiery darts of doubt and deception are aimed at you, which do you find the most challenging: trusting God's character, trusting God's promises and His word, or trusting God's program and His timing? Why? What biblical truth can extinguish those doubts and lies?

____

____

____

____

____

____

2. The helmet of salvation is the certainty of deliverance from sin and the protection of your mind in battle. How do you protect or renew your mind? After today's study, are there additional ways you want to renew your mind?

3. What are specific ways you guard your mind from evil? For example, are there movies, websites, TV shows, books, or music that you do not allow into your mind? Are there places you do not go or people you choose not to spend time with?

4. In Matthew 4:1-11, Jesus models how to use the sword of the Spirit. After today's lesson and reading this passage, how can you apply this in your life? What verses have helped you battle the enemy?

LIVE IT OUT

In today's teaching, Chip outlines five steps in engaging the enemy in spiritual warfare. We want to be fully prepared—ready with our spiritual armor on—to battle with the enemy at any moment. Read through the steps and take self-inventory. Write down how well you are doing with each step. Pray and ask God for His strength and wisdom in each of these steps:

1. Maintaining a healthy spiritual life.

2. Understanding your position in Christ—that you are a child of the all-powerful, living God.

3. Discerning when demonic influence is the cause of your struggle.

4. Claiming God's promises out loud.

5. Taking your authority and position in Christ to command demonic forces to stop their activity and leave.

THE INVISIBLE WAR

SESSION 7

The Christian's Secret Weapon

EPHESIANS 6:18-20

TAKE IT IN

The Missing Ingredient in Spiritual Warfare Is Intercessory Prayer

- **We are in an Invisible War.**

Finally, be strong in the Lord and in the strength of His might. Put on the full armor of God, so that you will be able to stand firm against the schemes of the devil. For our struggle is not against flesh and blood, but against the rulers, against the powers, against the world forces of this darkness, against the spiritual forces of wickedness in the heavenly places.

EPHESIANS 6:10-12 NASB

- **We are to prepare ourselves for battle.**

Therefore, take up the full armor of God, so that you will be able to resist in the evil day, and having done everything, to stand firm. Stand firm therefore, having girded your loins with truth, and having put on the breastplate of righteousness, and having shod your feet with the preparation of the gospel of peace.

EPHESIANS 6:13-15 NASB

- **When we resist the enemy, he will flee from us.**

...in addition to all, taking up the shield of faith with which you will be able to extinguish all the flaming arrows of the evil one. And take the helmet of salvation, and the sword of the Spirit, which is the word of God.

EPHESIANS 6:16-17 NASB

- **Intercessory prayer is pivotal and essential for corporate and individual deliverance.**

With all prayer and petition pray at all times in the Spirit, and with this in view, be on the alert with all perseverance and petition for all the saints, and pray on my behalf, that utterance may be given to me in the opening of my mouth, to make known with boldness the mystery of the gospel, for which I am an ambassador in chains; that in proclaiming it I may speak boldly, as I ought to speak.

EPHESIANS 6:18-20 NASB

Summary of Ephesians 6:18-20: The means by which believers are to withstand and overcome the attacks of the enemy in spiritual warfare is by consistent, intense, strategic prayer for one another in conjunction with the personal application of the armor of God.

1. **Intercessory prayer is our most powerful and strategic corporate weapon in spiritual warfare.**

   - Prayer has a direct impact on spiritual warfare.

And He said to them, "This kind cannot come out by anything but prayer."

MARK 9:29 NASB

   - Prayer provides and assists in the deliverance of others who are undergoing spiritual attack.

"Simon, Simon, behold, Satan has demanded permission to sift you like wheat; but I have prayed for you, that your faith may not fail; and you, when once you have turned again, strengthen your brothers."

LUKE 22:31-32 NASB

- Power falls where prayer prevails.

Acts 1:14; 2:42; 3:1; 4:24-35; 6:4-8; 8:14-16; 9:40-42; 10:1-4

2. What kind of prayer brings God's deliverance and power?

______________________________ **prayer**

"With all prayer and petition": all kinds of prayer

> **A: Adoration**
> **C: Confession**
> **T: Thanksgiving**
> **S: Supplication**

"Pray at all times": prayer on all occasions

______________________________ **prayer**

"Be on the alert": without sleep, vigilant

"With all perseverance": not giving up

> "Prayer is the battle, and the ministry is the spoils."—*Haddon Robinson*

______________________________ **prayer**

"For all the saints": that God's messengers will be bold

"Utterance may be given": that God's message will be clear and have opportunity

SUMMARY

The missing ingredient in most Christians' lives and in most churches is the commitment and regular practice of intercessory prayer. Scripture indicates that consistent, intense, and strategic intercessory prayer (individual and corporate) will in fact deliver us from the evil one.

"The great people of the earth today are the people who pray. I do not mean those who talk about prayer, nor those who say they believe in prayer, nor yet those who can explain about prayer; but I mean those people who take time and pray. They have not time. It must be taken from something else. This something else is important. Very important, and pressing, but still less important and less pressing than prayer."—S. D. Gordon

THINK IT OVER

1. Chip began today's session with a true story of a missionary who was working as a field medic in Africa. What thoughts ran through your head as the story unfolded and, one by one, the twenty-six men stood up? Does this man's story influence how you view the power of prayer? How?

____

____

____

____

____

____

2. Have you experienced a time when God brought someone to mind and you felt compelled to pray for that person?

3. Has God answered specific prayers in your life or the life of someone you know? How did God work?

4. What is intercessory prayer, and why is it our most powerful corporate weapon in spiritual warfare? Who can you meet with for prayer this week? Invite those God brings to mind for prayer and coffee.

5. What would it look like for you to develop a more consistent prayer life? Who do you know that could help you learn to pray more intensely and strategically? Ask to meet with them and learn from them.

LIVE IT OUT

The missing ingredient in our lives is often a commitment to consistent, intense, and strategic prayer. It is the means in which we can withstand and overcome the attacks of the enemy. We tend to pray small, self-focused prayers instead of big, God-centered prayers. This week ask God for big things that you know are on His heart, and watch what He does.

Practice the ACTS method of prayer this week, and with each step, write down what God brings to your heart and mind.

1. Adoration:

____

____

____

2. Confession:

____

____

____

3. Thanksgiving:

____

____

____

4. Supplication:

____

____

____

STUDY GUIDE

THE INVISIBLE WAR

SESSION 8

The Ministry of Deliverance

EPHESIANS 6:18-20

TAKE IT IN

The great majority of teaching in the Bible has to do with alertness, preparation, defense, and being proactive to prevent demonic influence from breaking our fellowship with Christ or thwarting God's program for our lives. However, what are we to do when the enemy gets a foothold in our lives, or in the lives of people we know and love?

The Ministry of Deliverance

Its Validity

- Jesus regularly exercised this ministry. *Mark 1:27, 39*
- The apostles regularly exercised this ministry. *Luke 10*
- The early church regularly exercised this ministry. *Acts 16*
    - Justin Martyr (c. 100–165)
    - Tertullian (c. 160–225)
    - Origen (c. 185–254)
    - Athanasius (c. 296–373)
- The New Testament writers provide clear direction concerning this ministry. *James 4:7-10*

Its Problems

- **____________________ and fanaticism tend to negatively color this ministry.**
- **____________________ concerning demon possession versus oppression of believers clouds the ministry's validity.**
- **____________ and __________________ have caused many to simply ignore this ministry.**

- **Those who engage in this ministry are often tempted by __________________ or become so singularly focused they fall into theological error.**

- **Assigning __________________ of all one's problems to demonic influence versus assuming personal responsibility and using biblical common sense call this ministry into question.**

The Causes of Demonic Influence

- Yielding to sin *John 8:34*
- Spiritual rebellion *1 Samuel 15:23*
- Strongholds in current Christian culture
  - Unforgiveness
  - Money
  - Sexual sin
- Participation in the occult *Deuteronomy 18:10-11*
- Unresolved anger and bitterness
- Association with those involved in satanic activity *2 Corinthians 6:14-16*

New Testament Evidences of Demonic Influence

- Severe sickness *Matthew 12:22*
- Divination (telling the future) *Acts 16:16*
- Unusual physical strength *Mark 5:3*
- Split personality *Mark 5:6-7*
- Resistance to spiritual help *Mark 5:7*
- Other voices from within *Mark 5:9*

The Cure for Demonic Influence

- Victory is through the cross of Christ. *Colossians 2:14-15*
- Victory is in the name of Jesus. *Matthew 10:1; Acts 5:16*
- Victory is in the power of the Holy Spirit. *1 John 4:4*

Specific Steps for Deliverance from Demonic Influence

1. For unbelievers, accept Christ. *John 1:12*
2. Confess sins. *1 John 1:9*
3. Renounce the works of the devil. *2 Corinthians 4:2*
4. Destroy occult objects. *Acts 19:17-20; 2 Chronicles 14:2-5; 23:17*
5. Break friendships with those involved in the occult. *2 Corinthians 6:14-16*
6. Rest in Christ's deliverance. *Colossians 1:13; Colossians 2:14-15*
7. Meditate on and apply God's Word. *Ephesians 6:17*
8. Engage in corporate prayer. *Ephesians 6:18; Matthew 18:19*
9. If necessary, exorcism in the name of Christ. *Acts 16:16-18*
    a. By a spiritually qualified counselor *Galatians 5*
    b. Who maintains humility *James 4:7*
    c. Who wears spiritual armor *Ephesians 6:12*
    d. Who knows the Word of God *Matthew 4:4*
    e. Who is supported by prayers of believers *Ephesians 6:18; Matthew 18:19*

THINK IT OVER

1. What first came to mind when you heard deliverance ministry? What extremes have you seen or experienced that caused you to question its validity?

2. Believers must choose between two opposite responses to the reality of the supernatural world:
   A. To respond in fear, living life on your terms, pretending the enemy does not exist
   B. To engage the enemy in victory because you are a child of the living God and want to make a difference

   What will you choose? What does it look like to trust God in this?

For the grace of God has appeared that offers salvation to all people. It teaches us to say "No" to ungodliness and worldly passions, and to live self-controlled, upright and godly lives in this present age.

TITUS 2:11-12 NIV

3. According to Titus, what does God's grace produce in our lives? What does it look like to live in both grace and purity, and how does that influence the way we interact with those around us?

4. Of the five ways listed in your notes, where are you most likely to knowingly or unknowingly open yourself up to demonic activity? What specific steps for deliverance do you need to apply to your life?

5. In light of all you have learned through this study, what do you believe is the one thing God wants you to do in His grace? Write it down, tell a friend about it, and ask for their accountability.

LIVE IT OUT

Putting on spiritual armor involves time, commitment, and intentionality. Below are a few ideas that could help you in your application of God's Word. Pick one, or think of another, and commit to following through.

Media Fast: Take a seven-to-fourteen-day break from all media. Spend that time reading the Bible and in prayer.

Additional Reading: Continue your learning on deliverance ministry by reading one or more of the books Chip recommended in this session.

Invisible War Review: Read through all the verses in the Invisible War study guide, and write out the ones that God impresses on your heart.

MEMORIZE EPHESIANS 6:10-20

Finally, be strong in the Lord and in his mighty power. Put on the full armor of God, so that you can take your stand against the devil's schemes. For our struggle is not against flesh and blood, but against the rulers, against the authorities, against the powers of this dark world and against the spiritual forces of evil in the heavenly realms.

Therefore put on the full armor of God, so that when the day of evil comes, you may be able to stand your ground, and after you have done everything, to stand.

Stand firm then, with the belt of truth buckled around your waist, with the breastplate of righteousness in place, and with your feet fitted with the readiness that comes from the gospel of peace.

In addition to all this, take up the shield of faith, with which you can extinguish all the flaming arrows of the evil one. Take the helmet of salvation and the sword of the Spirit, which is the word of God.

And pray in the Spirit on all occasions with all kinds of prayers and requests. With this in mind, be alert and always keep on praying for all the Lord's people. Pray also for me, that whenever I speak, words may be given me so that I will fearlessly make known the mystery of the gospel, for which I am an ambassador in chains. Pray that I may declare it fearlessly, as I should.

What's Next?
More Group Bible Studies from Chip Ingram

Balancing Life's Demands
Biblical Priorities for a Busy Life

Busy, tired, and stressed out? Learn how to put first things first and find peace in the midst of pressure and adversity.

Culture Shock
A Biblical Response to Today's Most Divisive Issues

Bring light—not heat—to divisive issues, such as abortion, homosexuality, sex, politics, the environment, and more.

Doing Good
What Happens When Christians Really Live Like Christians

This series clarifies what doing good will do in you and then through you for the benefit of others and the glory of God.

Experiencing God's Dream for Your Marriage
Practical Tools for a Thriving Marriage

Examine God's design for marriage and the real-life tools and practices that will transform it for a lifetime.

Watch previews and order at
LivingontheEdge.org
or 888.333.6003

Good to Great in God's Eyes

10 Practices Great Christians Have in Common

If you long for spiritual breakthrough, take a closer look at ten powerful practices that will rekindle a fresh infusion of faith.

Holy Ambition

Turning God-Shaped Dreams into Reality

Do you long to turn a God-inspired dream into reality? Learn how God uses everyday believers to accomplish extraordinary things.

Love, Sex, and Lasting Relationships

God's Prescription to Enhance Your Love Life

Do you believe in true love? Discover a better way to find love, stay in love, and build intimacy that lasts a lifetime.

Overcoming Emotions That Destroy

Constructive Tools for Destructive Emotions

We all struggle with destructive emotions that can ruin relationships. Learn God's plan to overcome angry feelings for good.

What's Next?
More Group Bible Studies from Chip Ingram

The Real God
How He Longs for You to See Him

A deeper look at seven attributes of God's character that will change the way you think, pray, and live.

The Real Heaven
What the Bible Actually Says

Chip Ingram digs into Scripture to reveal what heaven will be like, what we'll do there, and how we're to prepare for eternity today.

True Spirituality
Becoming a Romans 12 Christian

We live in a world that is activity-heavy and relationship-light. Learn the next steps toward true spirituality.

Transformed
The Miracle of Life Change

Ready to make a change? Explore God's process of true transformation and learn to spot barriers that hold you back from receiving God's best.

Watch previews and order at
LivingontheEdge.org
or 888.333.6003

Why I Believe

Straight Answers to Honest Questions about God, the Bible, and Christianity

Can miracles be explained? Is there really a God? There are solid, logical answers about claims of the Christian faith.

Your Divine Design

Discover, Develop, and Deploy Your Spiritual Gifts

How has God uniquely wired you? Discover God's purpose for spiritual gifts and how to identify your own.

Download the Chip Ingram App

The Chip Ingram App delivers daily devotionals, broadcasts, message notes, blog articles, and more right on your mobile device.

Get it on iTunes

ANDROID APP ON Google play

Download from Windows Phone Store

amazon apps Available on kindle fire